NORTHERN WEBSTER COUNTY

From The Air

JEC PUBLISHING COMPANY
2969 E. Chestnut Expy
Springfield, Missouri 65802
(800) 313-5121
www.jecpubco.com

Copyright © 2009 by Jason Rust

Library of Congress Control Number: 2009942119

ISBN: 978-0-9824801-8-2

Created by: Jason Rust

Photographs by: Jason Rust and Todd Revell

Prepared for Publishing by: JE Cornwell & Tom Dease

Printed in Canada

The first thing I can remember wanting to be when I grew up was a helicopter pilot. Helicopter pictures covered my walls and I had model helicopters hanging from the ceiling. However, like most childhood dreams, being a pilot was pushed to the side. The Lord blessed me with a wife, Geneine, and gave us two sons, Damon and Janson. He also began to bring people and opportunities in my path to help with reaching that childhood dream. At the age of 33 I received my private pilots license. What a joy it is to give family and friends their first helicopter ride. I love to fly over Marshfield and view my hometown from the air. I wanted to share this view with others so I solicited the assistance of friend and fellow co-worker, Todd Revell. He flew with me and took most of the pictures you will see in this book. I hope you enjoy the view as much as I do.

Jason Rust

To purchase any of the photographs in this book, and to view additional aerial photographs of Webster County, visit:

http://JasonRust.smugmug.com

MARSHFIELD, MO

Todd Revell

North of town, looking south.

SPEED LIMIT 40

THIS IS A *D.A.R.E* COMMUNITY

CITY LIMIT
MARSHFIELD
POP. 5,720

Jason Rust

Opposite page: Entering Marshfield on Hwy OO (Old Rt. 66). Above: Same view of Hwy OO from the air.

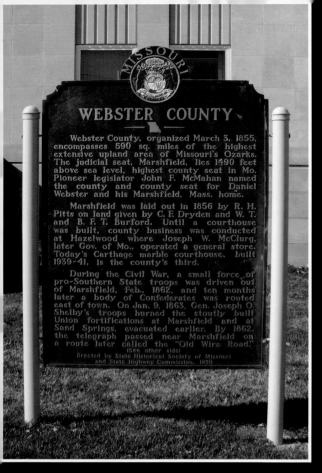

WEBSTER COUNTY

Webster County, organized March 3, 1855, encompasses 590 sq. miles of the highest extensive upland area of Missouri's Ozarks. The judicial seat, Marshfield, lies 1490 feet above sea level, highest county seat in Mo. Pioneer legislator John F. McMahan named the county and county seat for Daniel Webster and his Marshfield, Mass. home.

Marshfield was laid out in 1856 by R. H. Pitts on land given by C. F. Dryden and W. T. and B. F. T. Burford. Until a courthouse was built, county business was conducted at Hazelwood where Joseph W. McClurg, later Gov. of Mo., operated a general store. Today's Carthage marble courthouse, built 1939-41, is the county's third.

During the Civil War, a small force of pro-Southern State troops was driven out of Marshfield, Feb., 1862, and ten months later a body of Confederates was routed east of town. On Jan. 9, 1863, Gen. Joseph O. Shelby's troops burned the stoutly built Union fortifications at Marshfield and at Sand Springs, evacuated earlier. By 1862, the telegraph passed near Marshfield on a route later called the "Old Wire Road."
(See other side)
Erected by State Historical Society of Missouri and State Highway Commission, 1958

Marshfield and Webster County history as stated on a plaque, which is located on the East side of the Webster County Courthouse.

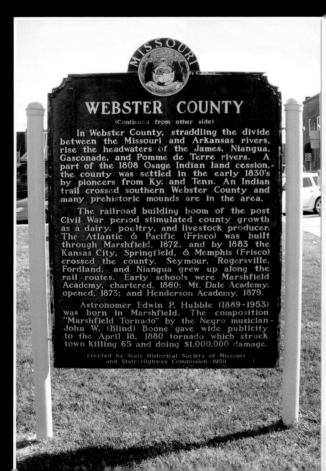

WEBSTER COUNTY
(Continued from other side)

In Webster County, straddling the divide between the Missouri and Arkansas rivers, rise the headwaters of the James, Niangua, Gasconade, and Pomme de Terre rivers. A part of the 1808 Osage Indian land cession, the county was settled in the early 1830's by pioneers from Ky. and Tenn. An Indian trail crossed southern Webster County and many prehistoric mounds are in the area.

The railroad building boom of the post Civil War period stimulated county growth as a dairy, poultry, and livestock producer. The Atlantic & Pacific (Frisco) was built through Marshfield, 1872, and by 1883 the Kansas City, Springfield, & Memphis (Frisco) crossed the county. Seymour, Rogersville, Fordland, and Niangua grew up along the rail routes. Early schools were Marshfield Academy, chartered, 1860; Mt. Dale Academy, opened, 1873; and Henderson Academy, 1879.

Astronomer Edwin P. Hubble (1889-1953) was born in Marshfield. The composition "Marshfield Tornado" by the Negro musician John W. (Blind) Boone gave wide publicity to the April 18, 1880 tornado which struck town killing 65 and doing $1,000,000 damage.
Erected by State Historical Society of Missouri and State Highway Commission, 1958

WELCOME TO
MARSHFIELD
HOME OF THE
BLUE JAYS

Jason Rust

Jason Rust

Jason Rust

Todd Revell

Todd Revell

Todd Revell

Jason Rust

EXIT 100

W | 38 Marshfield ↗

Interstate I-44
Exit 100

Todd Revell

Todd Rev

Todd Revell

Todd Revell

Todd Revell

Jason Rust

Jason Rust

Opposite Page:
Verteran's war memorial with a scale model of the Hubble Space Telescope in the background.

Above:
Mural of the history of Webster County.

Right:
Veteran's monument which was added in 2009. You will notice on the following page it is not present in the top two pictures.

Todd Revell

Todd Revell

Ellis O. Jackson
MARSHFIELD CITY PARK

Todd Revell

MARSHFIELD
ROTARY
PLAYGROUND

Todd Revell

Todd Revell

Todd Revell

Todd

Todd Revell

Todd Revell

Top Right:
MSU Observatory on Old Hillcrest Rd.

Bottom Left:
Frontier Theater and Amusement Park.

Bottom Right:
Unusual sight on Highway WW advertising
a salvage yard.

Todd Revell

Beckner's Airport, Northwest of town on Timber Ridge Road.
Marshfield's water towers are in the background.

Todd Revell

Camp Arrowhead, DD Hwy.

WELCOME TO NIANGUA, MO.

HOME OF THE CARDINALS

NIANGUA

Todd Revell

Todd Revell

Todd Revell

Todd Re

Todd Revell

Todd Revell

NORTHVIEW, MO

Todd Revell

Todd Revell

MARSHFIELD FIRE DISTRICT
NORTHVIEW STATION

Todd Revell

Todd Revell

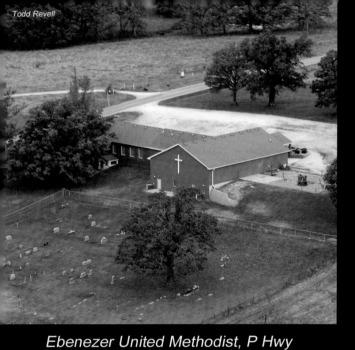

Ebenezer United Methodist, P Hwy

Timber Ridge Baptist. Off East 38 Hwy.

Pleasant View Church. West 38 Hwy.

Black Oak Free Will Baptist. DD Hwy.

Good Spring Baptist, HH Hwy.

Mission Home Baptist, W Hwy.

Todd Revell

Todd Revell

Todd Revell

Todd Revell

Todd Revell

Todd Revell

Corn maze at Gunter Farms, Hwy WW.

Corn m

Todd Revell

James River

James River

Kilburn Rd., Gasconade River

A Hwy, James River

KK Hwy, James River

Beach Rd., Niangua River

Bell Ford, James River

B Hwy, James River

Todd Revell

Opposite Page: ZZ Hwy (Rader), Gasconade River.
Above: Gasconade River.

Todd Revell

Todd Revell

Thanks to all my friends and family who assisted me in many ways with this project. Without your love and support this book would not have been possible.